Patience, Kindness, Goodness

Fruit of the Spirit

Lane Burgland

Contributions by Robert C. Baker

CONCORDIA PUBLISHING HOUSE • SAINT LOUIS

Written by Lane Burgland

Edited by Robert C. Baker

Prayers on pages 11, 25, and 46 adapted from *Family Prayers*, copyright © 1930 Concordia Publishing House; prayers on pages 17–18, 33, and 39 adapted from Gebets-Schatz *(Evangelical Lutheran Treasury of Prayers)*, copyright © 1894 and 1899 Concordia Publishing House, translated by Robert C. Baker.

Unless otherwise indicated, Scripture quotations are from The Holy Bible, English Standard Version, copyright © 2001 by Crossway Bibles, a division of Good News Publishers. Used by permission. All rights reserved.

Scripture quotations marked NIV are from the HOLY BIBLE, NEW INTERNATIONAL VERSION®. NIV®. Copyright © 1973, 1978, 1984 by International Bible Society. Used by permission of Zondervan Publishing House. All rights reserved.

Scripture quotations marked NKJV are from the New King James Version. Copyright © 1979, 1980, 1982 by Thomas Nelson, Inc. Used by permission. All rights reserved.

Scripture quotations marked NRSV are from the New Revised Standard Version of the Bible, copyright 1989, Division of Christian Education of the National Council of Churches of Christ in the United States of America. Used by permission. All rights reserved.

Scripture quotations marked KJV are from the King James or Authorized Version of the Bible.

This publication may be available in braille, in large print, or on cassette tape for the visually impaired. Please allow 8 to 12 weeks for delivery. Write to the Library for the Blind, 7550 Watson Rd., St. Louis, MO 63119-4409; call toll-free 1-888-215-2455; or visit the Web site: www.blindmission.org.

Manufactured in the U.S.A.

1 2 3 4 5 6 7 8 9 10   14 13 12 11 10 09 08 07 06 05

Contents

About This Series

By this My Father is glorified,
that you bear much fruit and so prove to be My disciples.

Jesus, *John 15:8*

Only hours before Jesus was arrested, He delivered an important message to His disciples (John 14–16). At the heart of this message He describes the "fruit" His disciples would bear, the works they would do to glorify the heavenly Father. Through the gift of the Spirit, Jesus promised love (John 14:21), joy (15:11), and peace (14:27) to them and to you.

However, many Christian families and congregations do not exhibit the fruit Jesus (and later Paul) described. Selfishness, pride, and abusive behavior arise all too easily for us. Sin is truly second nature to human beings, even to the people of God.

This Bible study series will help you produce the fruit God calls you to bear as a believer. Through biblical examples and teaching from both the Old and New Testaments, you will explore God's goodness and blessings for you in Christ. You will learn to crucify "the flesh with its passions and desires" and "live by the Spirit" (Galatians 5:24, 25).

Student Introduction

Good living begins with good understanding. For this reason Jesus spent considerable time teaching His disciples before sending them out in service. Among the things Jesus taught His disciples was "every healthy tree bears good fruit" (Matthew 7:17). In other words, God's people will naturally want to do His will by doing good works.

Unfortunately, Jesus' illustration about good trees bearing good fruit has been used as a reason to ignore Christian education about good works. The argument has been made that since Christians will naturally bear fruit and do good works there's no point preaching or teaching about them. There's no point in studying them. Just let nature take its course.

Certainly you and all God's people need to have confidence that God's Word and teaching will lead to good works. But no congregation can ignore the truth that the sinful nature is still very much at work within the people of God (Romans 7:15–19). You need constant pruning! Jesus also taught, "Abide in Me, and I in you. As the branch cannot bear fruit by itself, unless it abides in the vine, neither can you, unless you abide in Me" (John 15:4). He called you to cling to both the Law of His teaching (which commands good works) and the Gospel (which causes good works to grow).

The Work of the Spirit

When the apostle Paul wrote to the Christians in Galatia about the "fruit of the Spirit" (Galatians 5:22), he wrote to a congregation afflicted with sin. The Galatians had eagerly embraced the Gospel. But soon after the apostle left to preach elsewhere, the Galatians divided into factions and were carried away by false doctrine. They erred in the most basic ways by confusing God's Law and Gospel (3:2–3), attacking one another (5:15), and growing conceited (5:26; 6:3). They had lost the patience, kindness, and goodness first cultivated by the apostle's preaching. In response, Paul writes to them not only about correct doctrine (chs. 1–4) but also about Christian behavior: the fruit of the Spirit (chs. 5–6).

The list of the "fruit of the Spirit" in Galatians 5 is not the only list of good works recorded in the apostle Paul's letters. (See 2 Corinthians 6:6; Ephesians 4:2; Colossians 3:12; 1 Timothy 6:11; and 2 Timothy 2:22 for other examples.) Yet it is Paul's most complete list and is especially directed to congregational members rather than church leaders. In this list of nine "fruit," the apostle summarizes what Christ wants to cultivate in you by His Spirit.

You did not choose Me, but I chose you and appointed you that you should go and bear fruit and that your fruit should abide, so that whatever you ask the Father in My name, He may give it to you. These things I command you, so that you will love one another.
(John 15:16–17)

To prepare for "Patiently Awaiting," read Exodus 32.

1

Patiently Awaiting

Lord, please give me patience . . . and give it to me right now!

A prayer to receive patience immediately might seem silly, but it reflects our "hurry up/right now" approach to life. We prefer instant gratification to patiently waiting for something, even if what we are waiting for is better. For example, many lottery winners will accept a reduced monetary prize in order to have immediate cash, rather than waiting for the whole prize disbursed in annual installments. When it comes to suffering or doing without something we want, we show the same natural impatience. Commercials and other advertisements reinforce this attitude.

Paul lists *patience* as one of the precious gifts of the Holy Spirit in the Christian life. Like the other fruit of faith, patience grows from our relationship with God the Father through Jesus Christ, our Savior and Lord. We will turn to the Old Testament to learn something about the patience of God and then, in the New Testament, examine patience in the lives of God's people. Our study will conclude by exploring what the Bible teaches about the patience God gives through His Son.

1. Patience for one person may be considered impatience by another. What might Paul have in mind when he includes *patience* among the gifts of the Holy Spirit?

The Children of Israel

Parents might talk about how a strong-willed or mischievous child "tests" their patience. In that context, the child rebels against the parent, who then must figure out the appropriate response. Imagine you have told your child to stay away from the cookie jar until after dinner. Behind your back, she disobeys you. When you find out, how do you respond? If you do nothing, she will lose her respect for you. If you react in anger, you might punish her too harshly. Keep this scenario in mind as you read Exodus 32 and discuss the following questions.

2. In Exodus 34:1, God refers to a previous set of stone tablets on which He had written the Ten Commandments. What happened to them? (See Exodus 32:1–19.)

3. What did God propose to do to His people in response to their great sin in Exodus 32? Why didn't God do it?

4. How did God discipline them? (See Exodus 32:19–29; 35.)

5. What does Moses do that gives us an early picture of the cross of Christ? (See Exodus 32:30–34.)

Now read Exodus 34:1–7. The Lord "unpacks" His name for Moses in verses 6 and 7.

6. What do we learn about the Lord in these verses?

7. Compare several translations of verse 6 with one another. How do they differ?

8. Discuss the justice (righteousness) of God and the mercy (grace) of God in light of Exodus 34:7 and Exodus 20:3–6.

David's Trust

David offers us another example of an Old Testament believer who endured a great deal of trouble and hardship while still trusting God. His father-in-law, King Saul, tried to kill him on several different occasions, yet he refused to take vengeance (see 1 Samuel 19 and 23; compare 1 Samuel 24 and 26). Later, even one of his own sons plotted against him and nearly succeeded in murdering him (2 Samuel 15). Throughout his reign, David faced enemies within his own family and country and many from outside as well. In several psalms David turns to the Lord for help, acknowledging his own sin but trusting in God's patience and mercy. In Psalm 86, the center verse (v. 9) sets forth the theme of God's salvation for all people. This is the purpose of God's patience with sinners. God delays His wrath so that His plan of salvation in Christ Jesus might be accomplished and people from all nations, not just Israel, will come and worship Him.

9. Does David depend on his own good works as a basis for seeking God's help in this psalm?

10. David seems to think that an attack on him is an attack on God. Why would he think this (v. 14)?

11. How does God show His compassion, mercy, love, and faithfulness in being longsuffering (slow to anger)?

Job's Endurance

Job offers us a fascinating example of endurance in the face of terrible suffering. Read Job 1–2 and answer the following:

12. Who brought up the subject of Job?

13. What was the nature of Satan's accusation against Job?

14. What does Job lose and why?

Turn to Job 38–42.
15. Briefly summarize God's response to Job.

16. How does Job finally end up?

17. Had Job been patient? (See Job 3; 12:1–3; 16:1–3; 21:4.)

18. Did Job lose his faith? (See Job 19:23–27.)

O Almighty God, our heavenly Father, I humbly ask You to renew within me the gifts of Your Holy Spirit; increase my faith, strengthen my hope, enlighten my understanding, broaden my love, and make me always ready to serve You both in body and soul; through Jesus Christ, Your Son, our Lord. Amen.
(Henry Bernard Hemmeter, 1869–1948)

Sing "Let Us Ever Walk with Jesus" (*LW* 381; *TLH* 409).

Words to Remember

I waited patiently for the LORD; He inclined to me and heard my cry. He drew me up from the pit of destruction, out of the miry bog, and set my feet upon a rock, making my steps secure. Psalm 40:1–2

To prepare for "Patience as Love," read 1 Corinthians 13.

2

Patience as Love

Though patience be a tired mare, yet she will plod.

William Shakespeare, *Henry V*, act 2, scene 1

When Nym mentions patience to Bardolph, his comment seems to be in place. Lieutenant Bardolph has just brought up a grievous issue bothering the corporal. Nell Quickly, Nym's former fiancée, is now married to their mutual acquaintance, Ancient Pistol. They wait for Pistol's arrival at the Boar's Head Tavern in the seedy London district of Eastcheap. As they do, Nym contemplates the encounter with his former friend and what might be the result.

Bardolph's efforts to restore the friendship between Nym and Ancient Pistol, which will later include an "offer" to draw swords, exhibit a degree of patience. But so too do Corporal Nym's efforts to find a sense of closure to his now unrequited love. As Henry V's armies prepare to invade France, the patience of these three soldiers will be tested. War stands just on the horizon.

A variety of things may motivate us to be patient. Motivated by His love for us in Christ, God patiently deals with us, even though we do not deserve it. The same love that motivates God's patience moves us as Christians to be patient with others as well. As students of the New Testament, we can approach the subject of patience by means of both the Law and the Gospel.

19. What motivates us to patience on a human level? How does that compare or contrast with how we are motivated to patience as Christians?

Patient Forgiveness

Matthew records Jesus' story illustrating the importance of forgiveness (18:21–35). Peter asks how many times he should forgive another person. In terms strongly reminiscent of Lamech's prideful boast (Genesis 4:23–24) Jesus answers Peter and gives a concrete, if extreme, example.

20. How much did the king forgive the debtor?

21. How much did the fellow servant owe the man?

22. What did his refusal to forgive his fellow servant cost the man?

Patient Love

When Paul describes Christian love, he begins with "love is patient" (1 Corinthians 13:4). Pastors often use this chapter as a wedding text; however, Paul meant it to apply to all Christians in the body of Christ. Yet marriage offers a good venue to explore Paul's point.

23. Read through Paul's entire description of love in 1 Corinthians 13:4–8a. Share concrete examples of these elements actually at work in human relationships, especially in marriage.

24. Read Ephesians 4:1–6. What dimension does Paul add to patience in verse 2?

25. How does Christian patience preserve the unity of the body of Christ?

Patience in Suffering

James challenges his readers (then and now) to patience, especially in the face of persecution. While most Christians in the Western world do not face the kind of persecutions faced by James's original readers, hostility towards the Gospel and towards Christians continues in much of the world today as it did in the first several centuries of the New Testament era. Even in the West we can apply what James writes to situations we face all the time—crisis, stress, difficulties at work and at home, and the like. Read James 1:12 and 5:7–11.

26. What qualities develop in Christians when they face trials and temptations faithfully?

27. What is the "crown of life" in 1:12?

28. In light of James's comments in 5:7–11, why should Christians wait patiently for the Lord's return?

29. What qualities of the Lord do we depend on for our salvation, and how might we reflect these when faced with troubles of various kinds?

30. How easy is it to get angry with other people, even our loved ones, when we are under stress? How can we avoid that?

Patience While Delayed

How many times have we waited for someone's arrival at a specific time only to be kept waiting? Such delays create anger and frustration for those watching the clock. Jesus promised to return to judge the living and the dead. Some two thousand years later, we're still waiting. Is He *ever* going to return? Read 2 Peter 3:3–13.

31. What problem does Peter address in these verses?

32. Why did some people think Jesus would not return?

33. What seems like a long time to us does not seem so long to God. How does Peter make this point in these verses?

34. Why does Jesus delay His return to judge the living and the dead? (See 2 Peter 3:9, 15.)

35. What can Christians look forward to when Jesus returns?

Christ the Ideal

We find no greater example of patience, especially in the face of suffering, than our Lord Jesus Christ Himself. Throughout His ministry, Jesus showed tremendous patience with His followers (see Mark 8:14–33, for example). The one place where His patience shines most brightly, of course, is Calvary. If God's patience can be defined as delaying punishment and showing mercy, then the cross stands as the purest and strongest example. Read John 18–19.

36. Does Jesus have the power to stop the proceedings? Why does He choose not to do so? (See John 18:11.)

37. What indignities does Jesus suffer during the religious trial, and why does He endure it so patiently (18:19–24)?

38. What did His enemies accuse Him of in the religious trial? In the secular trial?

39. In light of Deuteronomy 21:22–23, how does the cross provide the perfect and ultimate example of longsuffering?

Dear God! Grant us also peaceful hearts and good courage in
our struggle and unrest against the devil, whom we cannot endure nor
finally defeat. We desire to have peace, and to praise and thank You, and
not to grumble nor become impatient against Your divine will. Grant
that peace in our hearts wins the day, so that we hold nothing against
You, our God, nor against our fellow man, because of impatience.

Rather, help us to remain calm and peaceful, both inwardly and outwardly, to You and to all people, until the coming of that final and eternal peace.
(Martin Luther, 1483–1546)

Sing "O God, My Faithful God" (*LW* 371; *TLH* 395).

Words to Remember

Know this, my beloved brothers: let every person be quick to hear, slow to speak, slow to anger; for the anger of man does not produce the righteousness that God requires. James 1:19–20

To prepare for "Kindness in Action," read the Book of Ruth.

3

Kindness in Action

In the end, only kindness matters.

Pop singer Jewel in her song "Hands"

That popular lyric might somewhat overstate the case, but it does seem that simple kindness is in short supply these days. Some communities have even tried "random acts of kindness" programs to increase good deeds in their area. Perhaps we are too busy, overwhelmed with the full schedules and demanding tasks from the workplace and at home. Perhaps we are too angry, plagued by road construction and aggressive drivers whenever we try to go somewhere. Maybe we are too stressed, pressed by payments and bills that never seem to get smaller or go away. Whatever the reason or reasons, kindness seems to have gone the way of the carrier pigeon or the dodo bird. You just don't see it anymore.

Kindness, as a fruit of the Spirit, stands out more sharply and becomes more important in such instances. The rare act of kindness draws attention, at least from the person who receives it. Kindness devotes time for others and sets aside the busy agendas that drive us mercilessly from one task to the next. Kindness reaches out to someone else if only for a moment. Kindness recognizes the personhood of the other, replacing the mannequin-like stranger with a real, living, human being whose life we touch through a simple act of thoughtfulness and consideration. It is true that more than kindness matters. But in the end (on Judgment Day) it is fair to say that kindness really does matter because it matters to God.

In both Testaments, kindness may be described as the practical application of compassion and mercy. Like the other fruit of the Spirit, God's own kindness models and shapes the kindness of His people.

40. Describe when you were particularly moved by an act of Christian kindness. What still stands out most vividly in your mind?

Psalms of Praise

In Psalm 31, David appeals to the Lord for help in the midst of a terrible conspiracy. Abandoned by his friends, he commits his cause entirely to God. (Notice v. 5, which Jesus quotes on the cross in Luke 23:46.) The first eight and last six verses each echo the theme of trust and set in bold relief the heart of the psalm (vv. 9–18). In verses 19–21, David praises God's "goodness" (v. 19), His protection (v. 20), and His "steadfast love" (v. 21, "kindness," KJV & NKJV; "wonderful love," NIV). In the end, David encourages not only his own soul, but also all God's people to trust in the Lord. God cares for His people and in His mercy rescues them. God's kindness is mercy in action.

Psalm 117 (the shortest psalm) calls the nations of the world and all its people to praise God. Why? He has shown great "steadfast love" (applied love) to us, and He continues to do so forever. His kindness, unlike so many human acts of kindness, sticks around. We can count on it. God is faithful to the promise of love implicit in His kind and compassionate intervention in history and in the lives of His people.

The author of Psalm 119 (the longest psalm) directs our attention to the Word of God and our response to it (both trust and obedience). He has suffered the Lord's discipline (see 119:67, 71, and 75), but he finds hope in one very important thing: God's kindness or "steadfast love" ("unfailing love," NIV) in 119:76. Discuss the following:

41. How do "kindness" (KJV, NKJV) and "steadfast love" (ESV) or "unfailing love" (NIV) differ from each other?

42. To what Scripture(s) do you turn when in pain or confusion?

43. What does God accomplish in our lives when He afflicts us?

Boaz and Ruth

Read Ruth 2 and 3. The author introduces Boaz in 2:1, a well-to-do relative of Naomi's late husband, Elimelech. Having returned to Israel from Moab, where Naomi and her family had moved due to an earlier famine, Naomi and Ruth find themselves in a very difficult situation. In order to provide even the bare minimum of food for survival, Ruth must follow the harvesters in the fields, picking up the individual grains and heads of grain that they left behind (called "gleaning"). Twelve or more long hours each day in the sun, bent over to pick up the grains, describes the gleaner's day of work.

44. What kindness did Boaz show to Ruth in chapter 2? Why?

45. In the Hebrew text, Ruth 2:20 stands in the exact center of the book and is the turning point of the story. What hope is born in Naomi's heart and why?

In chapter 3, Ruth approaches Boaz with a request.
46. What does she ask of Boaz?

47. How does Boaz respond?

48. What quality of Ruth's does he praise in 3:11?

49. What character quality do Ruth and Boaz share?

Read the conclusion to Ruth (4:13–22).
50. How does God reveal His character in this story?

51. What kindness does He show Boaz and Ruth?

52. Through Ruth and Boaz, what kindness does the Lord show the entire human race?

David and Mephibosheth

The background for David's kind acts towards Mephibosheth can be found in David's deep friendship with Jonathan, son of King Saul and father of Mephibosheth. Read 1 Samuel 18:3 and 20:14–17.
53. Who initiates the idea of making a covenant in both places?

54. What is a covenant, and do we have anything like it today?

55. How does Jonathan ratify his covenant with David?

56. What did a new dynastic king usually do to members of the preceding dynasty when he came to the throne?

57. What risk does Jonathan take in making this covenant with David?

2 Samuel 9 opens a section known as the "Court History of David" (chs. 9–20). Many years have passed since the death of Saul and Jonathan. David sits securely on the throne of Israel and now looks for a way to fulfill his covenant with Jonathan (see 9:1).

58. Who of Saul's family remains alive? Why?

59. What kindness does David show Mephibosheth?

60. What risk does David take by showing this kindness to him?

61. How does Mephibosheth end up? (See 2 Samuel 16:1–4; 19:24–30.)

62. What can we learn from this story?

The Model of Kindness

We turn now to two short passages that reveal God's ideal kindness, first to an individual and then to a nation. In both cases God's kindness flows from a covenant He made. Read Genesis 24.

63. What covenant had God made with Abraham (he refers to it in 24:7; see Genesis 12:6–7)?

64. What kind act does Rebekah do for Abraham's servant (24:19–20)?

65. How does this event reveal God's kindness?

Turn now to Isaiah 54. Here the prophet foretells the future glory of God's people won by the self-sacrifice of God's perfect Servant (52:13–53:12). God speaks in chapter 54 as His people's kinsman-redeemer (like Boaz in the Book of Ruth), especially in verses 5 and 8.

66. Boaz risked much in marrying Ruth; what does God sacrifice to redeem His people (see Isaiah 52:13–53:12)?

67. How is God's kindness to His people like His promise to Noah (Isaiah 54:9; see Genesis 9:11)?

68. According to Isaiah 54:10, which will last longer: the mountains or God's kindness ("unfailing love," NIV)? Why?

69. In your own life, how have you experienced God's kindness?

Father in heaven, You have taught us by Your Son to be merciful as You are merciful. At His cross we behold Your love, and our hearts are changed to be like Yours. With the mind of Jesus we are enabled to love our enemies, bless them that curse us, do good to them that hate us, pray for them that despitefully use us and persecute us, that we may be Your children, O heavenly Father. Grant that this mind may ever be in us. Without it we are not Yours. Father, hear us for Jesus' sake. Amen.
(Henry Bernard Hemmeter, 1869–1948)

Sing "My Faith Looks Trustingly" (*LW* 378; *TLH* 394).

Words to Remember

I led them with cords of kindness, with the bands of love, and I became to them as one who eases the yoke on their jaws, and I bent down to them and fed them. Hosea 11:4

To prepare for "Kindness Matters," read Matthew 24–25.

4

Kindness Matters

The kind see kindness; the wise see wisdom.

Chinese proverb

We tend to improve at those things we practice the most. Whether it's playing a musical instrument, spending our time with a sport or hobby, or exercising, our abilities improve through use and repetition. On the opposite side of the coin, if we do not practice or spend time doing an activity, our abilities will generally decline and perhaps disappear altogether. "Practice makes perfect," but no practice makes a mess.

It's also true that those things we practice frequently we also notice more readily in others. Guitarists and pianists will have their favorite musical heroes; they are admired for their ability and emulated in their style and technique. The same thing is true for the sport fisherman, needle worker, or long-distance runner. As the proverb says, we can see in others the ability or characteristic—such as kindness—we ourselves have and are attempting to bring to greater use.

70. God expressed His kindness toward us even when we were most undeserving. Review Titus 3:3–8. Paying attention to the verbs, write below how God expressed His kindness to us in Baptism.

Loving Our Enemies

As with the other fruit of the Spirit, we see in Scripture that kindness represents a very practical attitude and that it is shaped, formed, and modeled after a quality of God's own nature. Like the other fruit of the Spirit, we find that the kindness produced by the Spirit looks very different from what our sinful human nature would ordinarily produce. Read Luke 6:27–36 and discuss the following:

71. Contrast Christ's commands in 6:27–31 with how we ordinarily would react in those situations. How seriously should we take His admonition?

72. If you or your child must face bullies in the workplace or at school, how should you deal with them?

73. Can we actually live out the Golden Rule (Luke 6:31; Matthew 7:12)?

74. Describe the kindness of God as reflected in Luke 6:35–36. How far does God's kindness reach?

75. What ultimate purpose does God have in mind as He deals so kindly with people (see also Romans 2:4; 11:22)?

The Good Samaritan

The parable of the Good Samaritan presents a picture of kindness (undeserved love in action) that brings together many of the things revealed in our study so far. In Luke 10:25–37, notice how Jesus creates this story in response to the question offered by the expert in the Hebrew Scripture: "And who is my neighbor?" Jesus tells a story in which a man takes risks, refuses to count his personal costs in time, money, or inconvenience, and extends kindness even to his enemies. In doing so, Jesus shows us a perfect picture of the Golden Rule in action.

76. What type of relationship existed between the Samaritans and the Jews?

77. What did the expert in the Hebrew Scriptures hope to do by asking his question (v. 29)?

78. Why would a priest and a Levite pass by the injured man?

79. How would you measure the kindness of the Samaritan?

80. Can you come up with any modern parallels to this story? Discuss the pros and cons of helping strangers.

81. If the Samaritan's kindness reflects that requirement of God under the Law, who can justify themselves before Him on the Last Day?

Sheep and Goats

Jesus talks about the end of the world and about Judgment Day in Matthew 24–25. In the story about the sheep and the goats (Matthew 25:31–46), Jesus shows us why kindness matters. Using a scene familiar to His hearers, Jesus teaches them and us that kindness does not save someone on the Last Day but does provide public evidence of a private faith. Read these verses and answer the following:

82. Who is "the Son of Man"? (See also Daniel 7:13–14.) What gives Him the right to judge?

83. What indications do we have in this story that we are saved by grace through faith in Jesus Christ alone?

84. How do the kind acts of the sheep reflect their living faith?

85. How can Jesus say that those deeds done to Christians, even un-important ones, have been done to Him personally?

86. What terrible, evil deeds did the goats do to earn damnation?

87. For whom was hell originally created? Why do some people end up there? How can we make a difference?

The Gospel Spreads

In the Book of Acts, Luke records the story of the Gospel's advance within Jerusalem (chs. 1–7), into the Roman province of Judea-Samaria (chs. 8–9), and to the very capital of the empire (chs. 10–28). Chapters 3–4 tell the story of a miraculous healing. Peter heals a man who had been handicapped from birth more than forty years earlier. Unable to work, he had a permanent place near the favorite entrance to the temple compound, the gate called Beautiful. He had been a fixture there for such a long time and was so well known that everyone recognized the miracle, even those who were not happy with it. Read Acts 3:1–4:22 and discuss the following:

88. We sometimes think that all miracles depend on the faith of the sick or crippled person. Does Luke mention the beggar's faith prior to his healing in 3:1–10?

89. What similarities and differences do you notice between this healing and the miracle recorded in John 5:1–15? Note especially the different attitudes of the two men after they were healed.

90. What opportunity does Peter take when the crowd gathers in amazement (3:11–26)? What does the Holy Spirit accomplish through this speech (4:1–4)?

91. Toward what end did God use this "act of kindness" (4:9, NIV; "good deed," KJV and ESV)? In light of 4:12, why is this important?

The Lame Are Healed

In Acts 14, Paul encounters a man crippled from birth, much as Peter had helped in Jerusalem. However, Paul is in Gentile land. On his first missionary journey, Paul and his companions move through modern south-central Turkey to preach the Gospel. Read the story in verses 1–20 and answer the following questions:

92. What role does the crippled man's faith play? How did this man get such faith?

93. What did the townspeople think of Barnabas and Paul?

94. Paul manages to stop the crowd from making sacrifice to them and makes a point about the one true God. How, according to Paul, has God shown them kindness even in their ignorance?

95. How did Paul end up (14:19–20)? Is this an example of "no good deed goes unpunished"?

Christ the Ideal

In spite of their different reactions to similar acts of kindness, the Gentiles in Lystra and Derbe and the Jewish men and women in Jerusalem had one thing in common. They (and we) are all sinners wrapped up in ourselves, slaves to our mental, physical, and emotional desires. Kindness does not come naturally nor easily to us. Like the other fruit of the Spirit, the model for kindness is Christ Jesus. Read Titus 3:3–8 and talk about the following:

96. Paul pairs the kindness and love (literally, "philanthropy") of God in 3:4. When did these appear and how are they connected?

97. How does the kindness of God produce salvation?

98. Is God's kindness in Christ Jesus earned, or is it an undeserved gift?

99. What is the "washing of regeneration and renewal of the Holy Spirit" (v. 5)?

100. What happened to us in Baptism?

Ah, dearest Jesus, You chosen friend of souls! You proved Yourself kind to everyone during the days of Your flesh. Indeed You fulfilled what was long prophesied about You, that You would not be ill-tempered and cruel. How Your heart was full of love, Your countenance fair! How Your lips were gracious, Your eyes kind, Your gestures sweet, and Your hands helpful! By these You have left me an example, that I should express myself likewise to my neighbor. So grant me the grace that I learn such virtues from You and may follow in Your footsteps. Amen, kindest and gracious Jesus, amen.
(Nicholas Haas, 1665–1715)

Sing "How Can I Thank You, Lord" (*LW* 385; *TLH* 417).

Words to Remember

Put on then, as God's chosen ones, holy and beloved, compassion, kindness, humility, meekness, and patience, bearing with one another and, if one has a complaint against another, forgiving each other; as the Lord has forgiven you, so you also must forgive. And above all these put on love, which binds everything together in perfect harmony. Colossians 3:12–14

To prepare for "Goodness and Grace," read Psalm 23.

5

Goodness and Grace

The infernal Serpent; he it was whose guile,
Stirred up with envy and revenge, deceived
The mother of mankind.
John Milton, *Paradise Lost*, Book 1, 34–36

When the serpent tempted Eve in the Garden of Eden, he made seducing claims. He said that by eating the fruit of the forbidden tree Eve's eyes would be opened and she would then be like God, "knowing good and evil" (Genesis 3:5). No doubt this appeared to make sense to Eve, because God called the tree "the tree of the knowledge of good and evil" when he commanded Adam to avoid it (Genesis 2:9, 17). Eve took the fruit from the tree (the Bible does not tell us what kind of fruit it was) and ate. She shared it with her husband, Adam, as well.

Surely Adam remembered God's prohibition and threat: "But of the tree of the knowledge of good and evil you shall not eat, for in the day that you eat of it you shall surely die" (Genesis 2:17). Perhaps the fact that Eve did not immediately fall over dead or get struck by a lightning bolt from heaven convinced Adam that the serpent was right and God was wrong. Maybe Adam used Eve like a guinea pig, allowing her to risk her life while he silently maintained a "level of deniability." After all, he could always claim she acted on her own. Whatever the reason, he soon joined her in eating the fruit. As a result their eyes were indeed "opened." They now could judge "good" and "evil" on their own. Sadly, neither they nor we do a very good job of it.

101. When Adam and Eve ate the forbidden fruit, how "good" were the results?

Our Good Shepherd

Like many of the fruit of the Spirit in Galatians 5:22–23, goodness can include a broad range of things. We might think primarily of spiritual meanings for these gifts, but Old Testament writers frequently included material elements as well. Where we tend to divide human beings into body and soul and concentrate on the soul, the Bible looks at us as whole persons consisting of both body and soul. God interacts with us both spiritually and physically, and He provides for us both in this world and in the world to come. In Scripture we see the two parts of our human nature (spiritual and physical) woven together as one seamless tapestry. Read Psalm 23 and talk about the following:

102. Which blessings are distinctly physical?

103. Which ones might be mostly spiritual?

104. What do you think "goodness" (v. 6) means? Do you think it is primarily spiritual or physical?

The Covenant Connection

We might not have noticed it in Psalm 23, but "goodness" often has a covenant connection. Covenants, especially covenants between kings and their subjects, often ended in a banquet like the one mentioned in Psalm 23:5. Also, "mercy" (v. 6, KJV, ESV; NIV translates "love") often referred to the binding relationship established by making a covenant. The same covenant connection appears in another Davidic psalm, Psalm 27. Read through the psalm and then turn to 2 Samuel 7:8–16. Compare the promises God makes to David there with David's remarks in Psalm 27.

105. What did God do for David in 2 Samuel 7:8?

106. What did He do for him in verse 9?

107. What does He promise to do for him in verses 10–11a?

108. Which of these good things shows up most often in Psalm 27?

109. What do you think is the "goodness of the LORD" (v. 13) in this psalm?

The Glory of the Lord

The "goodness of the LORD" can mean much more than protection from enemies (David's emphasis in Psalm 27). Because of sin, God had severed fellowship with Adam and Eve, driving them out of the Garden of Eden and barring them from reentry (Genesis 3:24). No longer were people able to speak with God "face to face," as our first parents had done. Yet God did not abandon His creation. He continued to reach out to people. He rescued Noah and his family from the flood, and He established a covenant with Abraham. Through Abraham's descendant all the world would be blessed. However, apart from one encounter with Jacob (Genesis 32:30), God did not speak to a person "face to face" again until Moses. Moses, the servant of the Lord, had such a special relationship with God that only Jesus, the Son of God, held higher honor. (Hebrews 3:1–3 helps us see this.)

In Exodus 33, we get a glimpse of this special relationship between Moses and God and learn something about the goodness of the Lord. God sends an angel with Israel to drive out the enemies that will arise along the route of the Exodus (33:2). He tells them that He will not personally accompany them because of their sinfulness (33:5). This leads to the conversation in 33:12–23 between Moses, interceding for the people, and God, who reveals His goodness. Read Exodus 33:12–23 and discuss the following:

110. What concern does Moses raise in 33:12? How does God respond (v. 14)?

111. What does Moses use as the basis for his request to get God to go along with them personally?

112. What else does Moses ask for (33:18)?

113. What does God agree to do (33:19–23)?

114. Why can no one look on God's face and live?

115. How does God define His goodness (33:19)?

We thank God for His gifts, which we have received from Him. We ask that our dear Lord would henceforth grant us and feed us with His Word, so that we may be thereby satisfied. Ah, dear God, after this world You desire to grant us eternal life. Amen.

Glory be to God the Father, who created us. Glory be to God the Son, who redeemed us. Glory be to God the Holy Spirit, who sanctified us. Glory be to the holy and most blessed Trinity, both now and forever.

Amen.

(Torgau Catechism or Handbook, 1676)

Sing "We Sing the Almighty Power of God" (*LW* 441; *TLH* 43).

Words to Remember

For the LORD God is a sun and shield; the LORD bestows favor and honor. No good thing does He withhold from those who walk uprightly. O LORD of hosts, blessed is the one who trusts in You! Psalm 84:11–12

To prepare for "Goodness of God," read Romans 12–15.

6

Goodness of God

*Because indeed there was never law, or sect, or opinion, did so much
magnify goodness, as the Christian religion doth.*

Sir Francis Bacon in *Of Goodness and Goodness of Nature*

If Sir Francis's statement is true, then the Christian faith has practically cornered the market in extolling the virtue of goodness. Throughout the ages, and in spite of some evidence to the contrary, those calling themselves Christians have often made valiant attempts at doing good—not merely for themselves, but especially for others. In Christianity goodness is praised. Goodness is encouraged. Goodness is even urged upon those who may not desire to be good. Does that sound "good" to you? Does it at least sound familiar?

On the other hand, perhaps Sir Francis's words could be interpreted in this way. Maybe there is more to goodness than you and I, Christians even, are able to muster. Perhaps what constitutes goodness, what makes something good in and of itself, is more than what meets the eye. While we enjoy the people and the world around us, and call them good, maybe that is just too simple a conclusion. To amend Francis's phrase, maybe what Christianity really magnifies is Goodness Himself.

116. What criteria do you normally hold for determining whether someone, some thing, or some experience is good? How does Psalm 34:8 aid our understanding?

God and Good

Only God is good. That sounds a little strange to most people, but that's what Jesus says (Matthew 19:17; Luke 18:19). Health, safety, success, love, friends, and many other things fall into our category "good." But such may not be the case. Take our daily bread, for example. Certainly that would be good in anybody's book. Jesus even teaches us to pray to our heavenly Father for it (Matthew 6:11; Luke 11:3). Yet He also shows us that sometimes daily bread is not good. Read Matthew 4:1–4 to prepare for answering the following:

117. Review Exodus 16:1–4. When the Israelites entered the desert following their exodus from Egypt, they had to learn to trust God and obey Him. What did they complain about?

118. Look at Numbers 11:4–6 and 31–32. What did the Israelites complain about this time? How did God respond?

119. Read Deuteronomy 8:2–3. Why did the Lord put the Israelites through all this?

120. If daily bread is a good thing, why does Jesus resist it (Matthew 4:4)?

121. How was Jesus' temptation similar and yet different from the one faced by Israel in the wilderness? By Adam and Eve?

122. What does Jesus mean when He quotes Deuteronomy 8:3, "Man does not live by bread alone, but man lives by every word that comes from the mouth of the LORD"?

God's Law and Gospel

When God gave Israel His Law, He did not compose an arbitrary set of rules just for fun and games. The Law reflects God Himself as an expression of His holiness and righteousness. God reveals His will for our lives through the written Law in the Old Testament (see the Ten Commandments in Exodus 20 and Deuteronomy 5). By its very nature as an expression of God's holy will, the Law is good. So why do we have such terrible problems with the Law? Read Romans 7:7–14 and discuss the following:

123. If the Law is good, how can it produce sin (7:7–8)?

124. How can the Law, an expression of the living God, bring death (vv. 9–11)?

125. If sin uses the Law to create more sin, and if the Law kills us, is the Law good or not (v. 12)?

126. How does the goodness of the Law operate in our lives (v. 13)? How does the Law confront us with our standing as condemned sinners before a holy and righteous God?

127. What final and effective solution to Paul's predicament (and ours) under the Law does God provide (7:24–25)?

Practical Goodness

An abstract noun like *goodness* can be hard to visualize. We like more concrete nouns, words that evoke pictures and memories. When Paul lists goodness as one of the fruit of the Spirit (Galatians 5:22), we might easily pass by without seeing anything particular in our mind's eye.

In Romans 12, Paul helps us with the concrete, offering us a practical treatment of goodness. Romans 12–15 form something of a real-world application of his earlier chapters on Law, Gospel, the Spirit, and God's righteousness. He asks us to offer our lives as "a living sacrifice" (12:1), a happy contradiction of terms. Sacrifices become sacrifices because they are killed in a religious ceremony. A "living" sacrifice was impossible, yet Paul creates this image for us so that we have a quick, thumbnail sketch of the entire Christian life. Read Romans 12:1–21.

128. How is our mind transformed so we can test and approve God's good will (v. 2)?

129. What attitude comes with a transformed mind (v. 3)?

130. What metaphor does Paul use to convey the fact that goodness includes real fellowship with other believers (vv. 4–8)? What gift(s) do you have?

131. In the remaining verses (vv. 9–21) Paul lists a number of ways in which we offer ourselves as "a living sacrifice," including "hold fast to what is good" (v. 9). Which of these challenge you the most?

Christ the Ideal

In Jeremiah, the prophet calls the coming Messiah the "righteous Branch" (Jeremiah 23:5; 33:15). John the evangelist titles Jesus "the righteous" (1 John 2:1). The quality of righteousness reflects a right relationship with God, one built on trust and revealed in obedience to His will. We might suggest that goodness takes this one step further, providing a warmth and generosity that exceeds righteousness. Read Luke 18:18–30 and answer the following:

132. What "good things" does Jesus tell the rich young man to do (vv. 20–22)?

133. What are the odds of anyone, rich or poor, entering the kingdom of God on their own (v. 25)?

134. What event does Jesus have in mind in verse 27?

135. How much more does the goodness of God in Christ provide for His children (vv. 29–30)?

Holy Spirit, God with the Father and the Son, You bear witness among men, enlightening their minds, so that they may see God and know His salvation. Illumine also my heart and so lead me into all divine and saving truth. Show me Jesus, my Savior, in all His sufficiency and loveliness. Endow me with the grace that enables me to love God and to do His will. Sanctify my heart to be a holy temple for You, together with the Father and the Son, and inspire my soul with holy thinking and living. And to You, the Father, and the Son be praise and glory now and forever. Amen.

(Henry Bernard Hemmeter, 1869–1948)

Sing "Holy Spirit, Light Divine" (*LW* 166; *TLH* 234).

Words to Remember

For while we were still weak, at the right time Christ died for the ungodly. For one will scarcely die for a righteous person—though perhaps for a good person one would dare even to die—but God shows His love for us in that while we were still sinners, Christ died for us. Romans 5:6–8

Leader Guide

This guide is provided as a "safety net," a place to turn for help in answering questions and for enriching discussion. It will not answer every question raised in your class. Please read it, along with the questions, before class. Consult it in class only after exploring the Bible references and discussing what they teach. Please note the different abilities of your class members. Some will easily find the Bible passages listed in this study; others will struggle. To make participation easier, team up members of the class. For example, if a question asks you to look up several passages, assign one passage to one group, the second to another, and so on. Divide the work! Let participants present the answers they discover.

Some excellent hymns that may be sung at the opening of each session are "Almighty God, Your Word Is Cast" (*TLH* 49; *LW* 342), "Salvation unto Us Has Come" (*TLH* 377; *LW* 355), and "The Fruit of the Spirit" (*AGPS* 225).

1

Patiently Awaiting

Objectives

By the power of the Holy Spirit working through God's Word, participants will

- understand the nature of patience as an attribute (characteristic) of God and a gift of the Spirit in the Christian life;
- perceive the critical relationship between Christian patience and trust in Jesus as Lord;
- see the connection between patience (waiting for something) and endurance (surviving under pressure).

God's patience in the Old Testament refers to His willingness to delay punishment. The session leader should "connect the dots" for the class participants by explaining how God must punish sinners due to His righteous nature. God cannot ignore sin without violating Himself (this was the heart of Luther's struggle with the "righteousness of God").

1. The degree of patience we exhibit in various situations may depend on a variety of factors. In describing patience as a spiritual gift, Paul does not mean the degree of tolerance or civility we express by nature. Rather, he means that copious draught of patience drawn from the supernatural well of God-given faith. Faith exercises itself in love toward our neighbor (Galatians 5:6). Indeed, patience is love expressed to others (1 Corinthians 13:4).

The Children of Israel

2. Several months after the exodus from Egypt, God established a covenant with the people of Israel at Mt. Sinai. Yet in a very brief time

(forty days), the people turned from God to idolatry and gross immorality. Aaron and the Hebrew people were impatient in waiting for Moses' return from Mt. Sinai. When Moses finally arrived, he saw the calf and the people's carousing and threw the original tablets on the ground at the foot of the mountain (Exodus 32:19). Indeed, the people's impatience with the Lord and with His servant Moses had led them to "break" the Law of the Lord.

3. God reveals his patience in Exodus 32. Because of the golden calf incident and Israel's breaking of His covenant, God proposed to Moses to destroy Israel and build a new nation based on him. Moses intercedes for God's people, basing his appeal on God's promises to Abraham and Isaac. God does not break His Word, and Moses appeals to this integrity and God's mercy to save Israel from destruction.

4. Israel experiences God's discipline in the violent death of approximately three thousand citizens at the hands of the Levites and in a plague sent by God.

5. Moses' intercession in Exodus 32:31–32 previews the cross of Christ. He offers himself as a substitute for God's anger against Israel. Of course, such a sacrifice by Moses would not have earned forgiveness for God's people. Moses was no more than an ordinary human being. He was a sinner, himself deserving God's punishment (remember, he committed murder at one point). Only Jesus, truly God and truly man, can pay the Law's required penalty for sin as our substitute.

6. In Exodus 34:1–7, we learn a great deal about "the LORD" (Yahweh, "I AM") through what "the LORD said to Moses" (v. 1). God reveals Himself, among other things, as longsuffering.

7. By comparing various translations, the session leader can point out that "longsuffering" (as in KJV and NKJV) often may be more directly translated as "slow to anger" (as in ESV and NRSV). Other passages that reflect this revelation include Numbers 14:18; Nehemiah 9:17; and Joel 2:13. This highlights the nature of God's patience as a willingness to delay His wrath and punishment for the sake of His people. He passes over sins rather than treat them as they deserve—not because He is unrighteous (fails to keep His Word) but because He intends to pay the penalty Himself, in the person of His Son (the point of Romans 3:21–26).

8. By reading Exodus 34:7 and 20:3–6, we could almost say that the ratio of God's mercy to His justice is 333 or 250 to 1! (He punishes three to four generations but shows mercy to one thousand.) The session leader might also direct the students to Jonah 4:2. Jonah did not want to

go to Nineveh, because he desired their destruction. Knowing God to be gracious and patient, he figured that if the Ninevites repented, God would forgive them—the opposite of what he wanted.

David's Trust

This psalm of David constitutes a prayer for help in the midst of trouble. Note verse 7, where David affirms the privilege that every child of God has through faith to call upon the Lord in the midst of trouble with confidence that God will hear and answer. Asaph, one of David's choir directors, affirms the same truth in Psalm 50:15.

9. David turns to the mercy and grace of God as the basis for his appeal for help. As he had done when he sought forgiveness for sin (see Psalm 51), David trusts in God's grace.

10. Since he was anointed by Samuel at God's direction (1 Samuel 16), an attack on David constituted an attack on the Lord who appointed him king. The king represents God as he rules God's people.

11. At the point where the class discusses how the longsuffering nature of God reflects His grace and mercy, the session leader has the opportunity to lead participants to the cross. Simply delaying punishment wouldn't accomplish very much. Delaying punishment for the purpose of taking it on Himself (the whole purpose of the cross, Romans 3:21–26), on the other hand, reveals amazing grace and abundant mercy. God patiently waits for the cross (Savior) and calls His children to patiently trust Him, especially in times of trouble (Lord). He rescues us (Savior) and rules us (Lord).

Job's Endurance

James uses Job as an example of endurance (James 5:11) in a paragraph where he exhorts his readers to patience and trust in the Lord (James 5:7–11). The session leader can point out that trust in God as Lord (owner and ruler) serves as the foundation for patience and endurance in His people. If the patience of God reflects His mercy in delaying the outpouring of His wrath, the patience of God's people reveals a simple trust in God as God. That is, the child of God trusts God to know what is best and endures hardship, if necessary, while waiting for God to accomplish His purpose.

12. God broached the subject of Job in a discussion with Satan (Job 1:8). Job was a faithful child of God (v. 1) who practiced his faith daily (v. 5).

50

13. Satan charged Job with trusting in God because God "paid" him so well. Strip away his wealth and family, said Satan, and Job's faith will fail as well (vv. 9–11). When Job continued in his faith in spite of his terrible losses, Satan argued that Job would lose his faith if his health failed (Job 2:4–5).

14. God allows Satan to take Job's children, workers, and property. In a succession of four messengers (1:13–19), Job learns of losing his oxen, donkeys, sheep, camels, servants, and sons and daughters. See Job 1:2 for an inventory of Job's considerable losses.

15. When God addresses Job (chs. 38–41), God reminds him that He is sovereign. God alone is God, and only He has the right to make the kind of decisions about the world and its people that He makes. He is the owner and the ruler of all the universe. In short, He is Lord. Recognizing his sin (even in the context of his endurance and his faith), Job confesses his sin and receives forgiveness and restoration from God (ch. 42).

16. Following his friends' speeches and the Lord's rebuke, Job repents of wanting to know the mysteries behind God's sovereign actions. The Lord restores Job's blessings, including twice the number of livestock from each group of animals and the same number of children as had perished (see Job 42:12–13; compare to 1:2).

17. Throughout it all, Job continued to trust God—but not without serious complaint (Job 3; 12:1–3; 16:1–3; 21:4).

18. Job's pain and anger, depression and discouragement are real. But so is his faith (Job 19:23–27).

2

Patience as Love

Objectives

By the power of the Holy Spirit working through God's Word, participants will

- understand that God's patience toward us in Christ is motivated by His love and desire for our salvation;
- grow in our appreciation of God's forbearance toward us shown most explicitly in the cross of Christ, as we in turn exercise patience toward others;
- rejoice in the midst of trials and sufferings as we patiently await the return of our messianic King.

19. Factors affecting our patience with others may include our level of fatigue or our emotional state. We may desire to avoid conflict with others, and thus exercise "patience" because of fear of pain or reprisal. On a human level, there may be a variety of motivations for us to be patient with others. In Christ, however, patience is divine gift, a fruit of faith flowing from God's matchless and patient love for us in His Son. We love others—that is, we are patient with them—because He first loved us (1 John 4:10–11, 19).

Patient Forgiveness

20. The servant owed the king ten thousand talents. The session leader may want to translate this into more familiar currency. A talent was a measure of weight, eighty to one hundred pounds. Assuming the debt was measured in gold, the leader can take the current price of gold, multiply it by 16 (ounces per pound), multiply that number by 100 (the

number of pounds in a talent), and then multiply that number by 10,000. The figure is staggering, yet the debtor asks for the king's patience and, surprise of surprises, the king forgives him the entire debt.

21. The fellow servant owed him one hundred denarii (a denarius was a Roman silver coin), about what a common laborer would make in four months or so. Calculate the average working man's wage for that amount of time and you have a significant sum, although extremely tiny compared to ten thousand talents. He also asks for patience.

22. In the end, the debtor loses his forgiveness because he refused to forgive, perfectly illustrating Jesus' warning in Matthew 6:14–15.

The session leader may want to emphasize that God's patience, as demonstrated in the Old Testament portion of this study, operates for the purpose of salvation. God holds back His wrath so that Christ Jesus may take the sins of the world upon Himself. He calls us to act likewise, bearing patiently with each other. This includes forgiving as we have been forgiven. (See Luke 1:76–77; 6:37; 11:4; 17:3 4; 24:45–48.)

Patient Love

23. The study group will, hopefully, open up and share moments when Paul's description of love found concrete expression in their lives or in the lives of someone they know. The session leader will want to keep the focus on patience throughout the sharing but should be willing to let the discussion grow according to the interests of the group.

24. Paul's remarks in Ephesians 4:1–6 can serve to transition the group back to a more narrow exploration of patience. In verse 2, Paul defines it as "bearing with one another in love." The verb *bearing* appears in the present tense, emphasizing the ongoing aspect of Paul's point. Because we love each other as Christ Jesus has loved us, we are willing to endure other people's weaknesses, irritating habits, eccentricities, and the like. We hope they do the same for us. Unlike the servant in Jesus' story about forgiveness (Matthew 18), love motivates our patience.

25. Paul reminds us that together we form the one body of Christ and share in the unity of the Spirit (Ephesians 4:4–6). Because God loves us in Christ, we love God. Because we love God, we love His children (and patiently bear with all their imperfections). It may be possible for the session leader to offer anonymous examples of how families and churches have been divided over a refusal to bear with each other's weaknesses. At the heart of it, such divisions are a failure to love as we

have been loved and a practical denial of the unity we have in the Spirit through our Baptism (1 Corinthians 1; 3).

Patience in Suffering

26. The Greek word translated "trial" in James 1:12 can also be rendered "temptation." Some of the same virtues develop when we face trials in our lives as when we successfully battle temptations. The session leader could use human relationships as an analogy. We grow in our relationships with one another when faced with hardship, difficulty, temptation, and the like. At the heart of this picture lies trust. We trust Jesus as Savior and Lord.

27. The "crown of life" does not refer to the diadem of royalty (only Jesus wears that, Revelation 19:12—"many diadems" signifying absolute royalty and kingship). Rather, the "crown" denotes the garland or wreath won by Olympic champions in the games, equivalent to today's gold medals. The session leader could paraphrase "the gold medal of eternal life" when describing this to the group. A character that has been tested and proved faithful develops in the context of suffering and hardship, as Paul notes in Romans 5:1–5. Jesus won for us the "crown of life" on the cross, and we receive it freely at our Baptism. (The designation "crown of life" also appears in Revelation 2:10, another admonition to faithful living in the face of persecution with an eye to the final judgment on the Last Day.) In view of how the end of the world turns out, God asks us to wait patiently and trust Him as He works in the world.

28. That same picture serves as motivation for James's admonition in 5:7–11. Actually, James offers two reasons for waiting patiently for the Lord's return. First, Jesus will return *to judge*. Thus our waiting should not be marred by discontent or anger, because Jesus will judge that too (Law). Second, Jesus will return *for us*. Knowing how things ultimately turn out gives the Christian added strength to bear up under the present circumstance (Gospel).

The session leader might point out that stress often creates bad tempers. We find it very hard to be joyful, considerate, loving, and the like when problems and troubles come crashing down on us. James understands human nature very well. He calls us not only to wait patiently on the Lord, but also to do so with good humor and love for each other.

29. The qualities of compassion and mercy moved God to send His Son to the cross for our salvation. James asks his readers to show the same qualities towards each other, even when faced with suffering.

30. Answers may vary. With the Lord's grace through Word and Sacrament, each of us can learn practical and effective steps we may take, even when we're stressed, to express God's compassion and mercy toward others.

Patience While Delayed

31. Peter speaks to those who are faced with the taunt (itself a faulty conclusion) that since Jesus has not yet returned, He will never return.

32. Many early Christians expected Jesus to return within their lifetimes, or at least within one or two generations. When He did not, some turned away from the faith.

33. Peter reminds us of several things in this passage. First, God has the power to do anything He wants to do (He created the world, v. 5). Second, when God confronts a situation, He judges (He sent the flood, v. 6). Third, when Jesus returns He will judge all people (this time with fire, v. 7). Finally, God does not consider a few generations of mankind to be a long time (v. 8). The session leader should help the class understand that God does, in fact, know the difference between one thousand years and a day. The leader should also make it clear that Peter does not offer some sort of secret code where one thousand years = one day. He simply references Psalm 90:4 to make the point that for God one thousand years is not a long time, just like one day is not a long time from the human perspective.

34. Jesus delays His return to judge the living and the dead for one simple reason: He wants more people saved. God wants to give the population of the world time to hear the Gospel and, by the working and power of the Holy Spirit, to come to faith. He loves the world even though it opposes Him. He has commissioned the church to evangelize the world, which the church accomplishes through baptizing and teaching (Matthew 28:18–20).

35. When Jesus returns, Christians can look forward to a resurrection to eternal life and a new heaven (the original is plural, reflecting the dual form of the Hebrew—"[two] heavens" represents the day sky and the night sky, as in Genesis 1:1) and a new earth! Once again a New Testament writer calls his readers to patient waiting, motivated by the knowledge of how things will turn out in the end. Trust the Lord to know what He is doing, and understand that His passion is saving people.

Christ the Ideal

The student has already seen something of Scripture's witness to God's patience, especially in the Old Testament section of this study. In John 18–19, we see a concrete demonstration of this patience (1) motivated by love, (2) delaying punishment, and (3) for the sake of salvation. Jesus heads to the cross, for this is the cup (a symbol of suffering; see Mark 10:38–39) given Him by the Father, as He explains in John 18:11.

36. Of course, Jesus has the power to stop the proceedings, just as He had the power to avert any of the actions against Him. But out of love for all mankind He allows them to proceed, suffering injustice for our sakes. In John 18:11, Jesus commands Peter to abstain from using earthly power to defend Him, for His humiliation, suffering, and death is the will of the Father ("the cup that the Father has given Me," John 18:11). Likewise Christians do not use force to defend Christ or His Gospel, but rather suffer all manner of indignities and persecutions for His sake in the faithful proclamation of His name (Matthew 5:10–11).

37. Besides the inherent rudeness of the religious leaders and in spite of Jesus' cooperation and truthfulness, John records our Lord out of love for us being physically abused by a temple guard in the presence of the high priest.

38. In the religious trial, Jesus was accused of blasphemy because He claimed to be the Messiah even though He seemed to have none of the credentials for that title. In the first century A.D., the term *blasphemy* was broad enough to include such a situation. In the secular trial under Pilate, Jesus stood accused of claiming to be king without Caesar's authorization, a capital offense. Ironically, He was (and is) both Messiah and King. Jesus goes to the cross as the messianic King and hangs under the title "Jesus of Nazareth, King of the Jews."

39. Deuteronomy 21:22–23 gives instructions regarding the implementation of punishment for capital crimes for the people of Israel. In Christ's cross, we see the perfect and ultimate example of God's long-suffering through His Son. First, His patient forbearance had left sins unpunished prior to Calvary (see Romans 3:21–26, especially v. 25). The suspended sentence against sinners was finally carried out on Good Friday. Second, Jesus patiently bears all that He suffers because the Father wills it and we need it. Out of His great love for us, and for the sake of our salvation, He withholds His anger and justice against those who accuse, abuse, mock, and crucify Him. At the cross we learn that the long-suffering (or patience) of God operates for the salvation of sinners. We

also see what it means to bear patiently with others, especially those who persecute us. In imitation of Christ, God calls us to demonstrate the same longsuffering (patience) toward others. Do not get angry with those who hurt you, we might say, because Christ gave His life for us on the cross and did not respond in anger to those who abused Him, even though they pounded spikes into His wrists and feet (see Luke 23:34).

3

Kindness in Action

Objectives

By the power of the Holy Spirit working through God's Word, participants will

- develop an appreciation for kindness as an outworking of faith in daily life;
- understand how God's kindness in Christ Jesus serves as the model for shaping our attitudes towards others;
- realize the importance God places on our acts of kindness, reflected in the final judgment.

40. All of us have stories in which the kindness of another has deeply impressed us or has been a source of great blessing. Participants may voluntarily share their experiences in smaller groups then decide which story to share with the larger group.

The session leader might consider extending the opening of this session by asking the participants whether they think kindness is less common than in the past. If so, what caused the decline? The leader can move the discussion to the subject of values systems. For example, which is more important—that we arrive on time at our destination or that we render aid to someone in need on the side of the road along our way? The leader will also want to ask what role risk plays when or how we decide to help others on the roadside and whether technology (cell phones, etc.) have made our decisions any easier.

The leader should remind the participants that one English word might translate several different Greek and/or Hebrew words and vice versa. For example, the Greek word translated by the NIV in Galatians 5:22 as "kindness" often appears in the Greek Old Testament (the Septuagint) as the choice to translate "good" or "goodness." Translators of the KJV and NKJV, on the other hand, often use "kindness" to translate "mercy" or "covenant love." The instructor should tell the students that we are studying the concept of kindness as it appears in Scripture and that some translations will use different English words to express a shade of meaning or nuance in the word used by the original author. Translations may not agree with each other, but, as the session leader can point out, most translations communicate the same general idea in each verse studied.

Psalms of Praise

In Psalm 31, the session leader should move the participants to verses 20–24 (eight stanzas in Hebrew that resound the theme of trusting in God). David praises God's goodness (the Greek Old Testament uses the same word here as Paul uses in Galatians 5:22, translated there as "kindness"). The KJV and NKJV use "marvelous kindness" in verse 21 ("wonderful love" in the NIV) to describe God's intervention in his predicament (boldly described as a "besieged city"). The point: God's character ("goodness") coupled with His attitude towards His people ("mercy") leads Him to concrete action ("wonderful kindness").

Psalm 117 is a short "praise" psalm (in Hebrew, "hallelujah") that echoes the other praise ("Hallel") psalms (113–118). Customary in Hebrew poetry, the psalmist says what he wants to say in the first half of the verse and then repeats the theme in the second half of the verse, often adding a thought or variation for emphasis. In 117:1, the author calls all the nations and people of the earth to praise and extol God. In 117:2, he tells us why we should do so: God has shown "steadfast love" or kindness (NIV "love") toward us, and His "faithfulness" endures forever. In other words, we can count on God's kindness at all times. He won't withdraw it suddenly, even if we deserve for Him to do so.

The author of Psalm 119 drives home the same point about God's kindness. He understands that God's kindness flows from God's love for His people and the promise of salvation that He has made to those who trust in Him. The "promise" of the NIV in 119:76 might mislead the English reader a bit. The author bases his confidence on God's Word. This might be a personal communication to the author, but given the psalmist's emphasis on the written Word throughout the psalm, he most likely has in mind the Holy Scripture. In the midst of his suffering, the psalmist finds comfort and confidence in God's Word because in that

Word God reveals His kindness ("steadfast love" in action). Note the following:

41. "Kindness" often denotes concrete action; "steadfast" or "unfailing" love commonly refers to an attitude or disposition.

42. Answers will vary. Participants may be willing to share some Bible passages that have meant a lot to them in times of trial (for example, Psalm 23; Psalm 130; and Romans 8:28–39). Scripture holds out the numerous and comforting promises of God's work and presence with us through our pain and affliction.

43. Through affliction God corrects us when we are wrong, builds our faith, teaches us to trust Him in spite of what's going on in our lives, shows our faith to others, and drives us further into the Scriptures (see Psalm 119:67 and 71 for the first and last of these valuable benefits God produces through our suffering).

Boaz and Ruth

This session addresses other aspects of the Book of Ruth not covered in *Love, Joy, Peace*. The session leader will want to become familiar with the agricultural practice of gleaning in order to provide a picture for the participants of Ruth's predicament. Ruth gave up her family, tribe, and clan in order to follow Naomi. We often have little idea what this meant. She left a life where she had some hope of remarriage, a future family, protection within an extended family, and a place in her community. In Israel she was an outsider, a Moabitess, a foreigner who was fair game for anyone who wished to victimize her. She would have no hope of marriage or family, no place in the community, no protection within a tribe or clan or family. She would have to work very long hours (72–80 hours per week) picking up grains in the field just to survive. The leader should impress on the students the cost of Ruth's devotion to Naomi and the life she chose in order to be with her.

The session leader should also explain the practice of levirate marriage (see Genesis 38:8; Deuteronomy 25:5–6). This law plays a critical role in Boaz's actions in chapter 4. When the nearest relative ("kinsman-redeemer") married the widow of his deceased family member, the first child born to that union had the legal status of the dead man's child. That child would then inherit the deceased person's property and, as a near relative of the biological father, would have a legal claim on the biological father's property (depending on that man's legal heirs). This means that Boaz risked a great deal in marrying Ruth and highlights one of the very important aspects of kindness: it is willing to take risks (a point made in the story of the Good Samaritan, Luke 10).

44. Boaz shows great kindness to Ruth (and by extension to Naomi) by providing a safe working environment for her, giving her more food than she would otherwise have gleaned, and having the harvesters "plant" extra grain for her. He does this because her sacrifice for Naomi has deeply impressed him (2:11–12). While many men respond simply to a woman's physical appearance, Boaz sees beyond the surface and into the rich character of her heart.

45. Boaz's kind actions open Naomi's eyes to the kindness of the Lord. God acts through Boaz, a kinsman-redeemer, to grant an heir for Naomi's deceased husband and a husband for her daughter-in-law— relieving them of the desperate poverty and vulnerability they had faced. God acted in mercy to provide for both the living (Naomi and Ruth) and the dead (the late Elimelech and his sons).

46. In chapter 3, Ruth, directed by Naomi, approaches Boaz and asks him to fulfill his role as kinsman-redeemer. She asks for marriage in verse 9.

47. Boaz responds positively to Ruth's request in verse 11, praising her character.

48. The author of the book had used the same Hebrew word translated in verse 11 for a "worthy woman" ("worthy," NRSV; "virtuous, KJV") in 2:1 to describe Boaz ("man of standing," NIV; "prominent," NRSV; "mighty," KJV). The session leader can make the point that a person's actions reveal the underlying character of that individual.

49. The author of Ruth introduces us to two very remarkable people (Ruth and Boaz) who share a common character quality: kindness to others.

50. In chapter 4, the author concludes the story of Ruth with a genealogy. God reveals His character by showing great kindness to the living and the dead, as Naomi said in 2:20.

51. God grants a child to Ruth and Boaz, a child who became an ancestor of David and through David, an ancestor of Jesus Christ.

52. The leader can direct the participant's attention to Matthew's genealogy in Matthew 1:5 where Ruth, a Moabitess, is mentioned by name. (Note: Matthew names four women, each of them a "problem" from the Jewish perspective, demonstrating God's grace throughout the whole history of His people.) The leader may also want to point out that the New Testament writers viewed the birth, life, ministry, death, and resurrection of Jesus as a demonstration of God's "kindness" (as Paul

writes in Titus 3:4). "Kindness" describes concrete acts that reveal a person's character and heart, setting aside personal welfare and taking risks for the benefit of others.

David and Mephibosheth

53. In both passages Jonathan initiates a covenant with David. (Note also that Jonathan makes [literally "cuts"] a covenant with David in 1 Samuel 18:3.) At the time, Jonathan was socially superior to David. He was King Saul's son, a member of the royal family, and David was merely a soldier in the army. Yet Jonathan and David's friendship bridged the social gap and their loyalty remained strong even though upcoming events would make their friendship very difficult.

54. The closest thing to a covenant that we have today is a contract. Yet covenants, especially the kind of covenant Jonathan makes with David, have several distinct features. The socially superior sets all the terms of the covenant—there are no negotiations. Similar to the "Royal Grant" covenant (see p. 18 of the *Concordia Self-Study Bible*), Jonathan's covenant with David is unconditional. David does not have to do anything to receive or maintain Jonathan's pledge.

55. Jonathan ratifies his covenant with David by giving David his robe, sword, bow, and belt (1 Samuel 18:4). Because Jonathan (and his father, Saul—see 1 Samuel 18:12) knew the Lord was with David, he may have understood that David would be the next king.

56. Among many nations a new dynastic king usually killed all relatives of the previous dynasty upon coming to power. Jonathan's interest in making a covenant with David certainly reflects his deep love for his friend, but it may also contain a plea for kindness when David becomes king. Jonathan's concern for his own family surfaces in 1 Samuel 20:14–15. Realizing that Saul's hostility toward David would eventually lead to Saul's destruction, Jonathan asks for kindness ("steadfast love").

57. Jonathan takes a terrible risk by making a covenant with David. If King Saul were to find out, Jonathan's life would certainly have been forfeit even though he was Saul's son (much as Saul killed the priests at Nob for helping David—see 1 Samuel 21:1–9; 22:6–19). David would not kill Jonathan nor would he harm his family (including King Saul). Ironically, Jonathan's life stands at risk from the family he has asked David to protect!

58. As the reader turns to 2 Samuel 9, we read that David remembered his covenant with Jonathan and looked for some way to fulfill his promise to his dear friend. The author of 1 and 2 Samuel introduces us to Mephibosheth in 2 Samuel 4:4. No one considers him a viable candidate for king because he had been injured as a child and suffered from a physical disability (crippled feet). Mephibosheth had been five years old when his father, Jonathan, died on the battlefield. By the time we read about him in 2 Samuel 9, he has a young son of his own (9:12). He survived because his nurse spirited him away as a child. He continued to survive because he was physically handicapped as a result of an accident during that flight with his nurse. Crippled as he was, he posed no serious threat to David.

59. David shows great kindness to Mephibosheth by recalling him to the capital, restoring his lands to him (9:7), and establishing his social position as equal to his own family (eating at David's table).

60. By treating Mephibosheth with extravagant kindness, David ran the risk that a direct descendant in the former dynastic line might rise up against him to reclaim the throne.

61. The session leader may want to share with class participants that Mephibosheth acted foolishly in the years ahead, dreaming of becoming king and losing the lands back to Ziba, his servant (read the sad story in 2 Samuel 16:1–4; 19:24–30).

There is an old saying: "No good deed goes unpunished." In the case of David and Mephibosheth, this seems to be true. Mephibosheth apparently returns David's kindness by harboring a desire to become king himself, as impossible as that would have been. When David fled Jerusalem because of Absalom's attempt to overthrow him, Mephibosheth thought he had a chance to be king (so his servant Ziba reported to David). After Absalom's death and David's return to Jerusalem, Mephibosheth tries to blame Ziba for his own actions. His excuse has the same weight and credibility as when a students cries, "The dog ate my homework."

Still, in 19:30, Mephibosheth declines half of the property that had been given to the servant Ziba for Ziba's loyalty to David in his flight from Jerusalem. Perhaps Mephibosheth figured he was better off not pushing his luck. In any event, we leave him in a situation very much like we found him—cut off from the rich and powerful, forgotten by the movers and shakers, virtually alone. The final mention of Mephibosheth is in 21:7, where David spares his life. Throughout it all, David kept his promise, showed kindness to Jonathan's family even though it meant taking risks, and proved loyal to his deceased friend and the promise he made.

62. The session leader can discuss what participants can learn from the story of David and Mephibosheth. We see kindness as a concrete act of love in these events. David loved Jonathan and showed kindness to his family in the person of Mephibosheth. (Don't confuse Mephibosheth, son of Jonathan, with Mephibosheth, son of Saul, executed by the Gibeonites in 2 Samuel 21:1–9.)

We see kindness take risks, as David allowed a potential rival for his throne (albeit a highly unlikely one due to his physical impairment) to live and even brought him to Jerusalem, "adopting" him into his own family.

We also see kindness spurned, as Mephibosheth turns away from David's mercy and compassion to seek his own agenda. Kindness acts unilaterally. That is, like undeserved love it does not require a positive response to validate itself. Kindness acts because the person who shows kindness acts on unconditional love.

The Model of Kindness

63. God promised to make Abraham a great nation and to bless all nations through his Seed. This promise also included at this time the land upon which Abraham's physical descendants would live.

In Genesis 24, Abraham's servant searches for a wife for Isaac, Abraham's son born to the promise (Genesis 12:1–3; 17:19; 21:12). Abraham carefully instructs his servant on the girl's qualifications and insists that she be willing to relocate to the land promised him by the Lord. She must be related to Abraham as well. Abraham and Sarah, his wife, were half brother and sister (Genesis 20:12). Isaac, their son, married his father's grandniece, Rebekah (Genesis 24:15). Their son Jacob married two first cousins on his mother's side, Leah and Rachel. The practice of marrying within the extended family is known as "endogamy" and was widely practiced in Abraham's day—although it is largely forbidden in the Mosaic Law (as in Leviticus 18, for example).

64. Rebekah goes beyond the call of duty when she offers to water the servant's camels. Her act of generosity and hospitality revealed her character, a personality and temperament well suited for life in Abraham's household.

65. By this kind act, God reveals to Abraham's servant the right woman for Isaac—and, in doing so, God has kept His promise and covenant.

66. In Isaiah 54, God reveals His grace to His people through the sacrifice of His Servant (52:13–53:12). As a result of that Servant's death for their sins, God reconciles them to Himself. Boaz risked his estate to redeem Ruth. God pays a much higher price to redeem His beloved: the death of His Son.

67. Isaiah sounds a tremendous note of comfort in 54:9 when he quotes God as saying His kindness will never end. "Never again" echoed in Genesis 9:11 regarding the flood waters. Now "never again" will God be angry or rebuke His people.

68. God's kindness will outlast even the mountains because it is based on His promise, His "covenant of peace" made with His people through the perfect Servant.

The session leader will want to remind the participants that the ancients "cut covenant," that is, they sacrificed an animal to seal the promise in the blood of the sacrificial victim. In God's covenant with His people, the sacrificial victim is His Son, Jesus Christ. (See John 1:29–34; Revelation 5:6–14.)

69. In answering the last question, the session leader will want to direct participants to the cross of Christ as God's greatest kindness to us. The New Testament study will lead the participants in this direction and try to make the connection between God's promise of salvation (His "covenant of peace") and His great grace (kindness = undeserved love in action).

4

Kindness Matters

Objectives

By the power of the Holy Spirit working through God's Word, participants will
- acknowledge God's unfathomable kindness in Christ toward all people, which extends even toward His enemies, the ungrateful, and the wicked;
- reflect on the kindness of the Good Samaritan, which is ultimately personified by Christ Himself;
- see in our Baptism into Christ the connection between kindness and love, and resolve to exercise toward others God's love given to us in this Sacrament.

70. Titus 3:3–8 is filled with rich imagery describing God's kindness toward us through His Son. Leaders may direct participants to pay close attention to the verbs in these verses by asking, Who is doing the action? What is being done? In Baptism God saved us (mentioned twice in v. 5), generously poured the Holy Spirit out on us (v. 6), justified us by His grace (v. 7), and made us heirs of eternal life (v. 7). All in all, this Sacrament expresses and effects God's kindness in Christ in a most profound and concrete way.

Loving Our Enemies

The Greek word translated by the ESV in Galatians 5:22 as "kindness" (KJV "gentleness") occurs only sixteen times or so in the New Testament. Luke 6:27–36 "unpacks" kindness by giving the reader a practical example of God's kindness. The session leader can point out three characteristics of kindness based on this passage: (1) Kindness produces generosity; (2) Kindness can be summarized in the Golden Rule; (3) Kindness embraces all people, including enemies, the ungrateful, and the wicked.

71–73. The leader can direct the discussion of Luke 6:27–36 by first asking if Jesus' admonitions here are practical. Can a Christian actually obey Jesus in the real world of the living room, the workplace, or the school ground?

While the answer is yes, class participants should be encouraged to address the questions in such as way as to struggle with the conflict between self-preservation and Christ's commands in this section (see also the Sermon on the Mount, Matthew 5–7).

74. Luke 6:35–36 highlights the inclusive nature of God's mercy. He sends rain both upon the just and the unjust, providing daily bread for billions who neither acknowledge nor obey Him. The session leader can begin to help the participants understand that the spiritual gift of kindness in Galatians 5:22 reaches out to all people, not just to family, friends, and neighbors of proximity (a point Jesus also makes in Matthew 5:43–48).

75. In Romans 2:4 and 11:22, God reveals His ultimate purpose in acting kindly towards people—He wants people to repent and turn in faith to Christ as Savior and as Lord.

The Good Samaritan

No one can match God's kindness. Who can achieve perfect love for all things, including enemies and persecutors? Yet as we read in Luke 6:47 and Matthew 5:48, God's Law requires us to meet God's own standard of perfection and mercy. The story of the Good Samaritan drives this point home with a vivid illustration of an act of kindness that might be possible but would almost certainly never have happened in reality.

76. Samaritans and Jews were bitter enemies, heirs of a centuries-long tradition of hatred and animosity. These feelings were strong and existed on both sides. For readers aware of the deep and abiding hatred shared by these neighbors, this parable packs extra punch. If the session leader has time, it would be worthwhile to research the origin and history of the Samaritans in a good Bible dictionary, encyclopedia, or online.

77. The expert in the Hebrew Scriptures hoped to justify himself (v. 29). In other words, he wanted to defend his life and conduct before God based on his performance of the Law. However, we have seen that God's standard for our behavior is the same standard He sets forth in His own great kindness to *all* people. By telling this parable and by the brief conversation that follows (vv. 36–37), Jesus completely dismantles the Bible scholar's self-righteousness. Not even someone as devoted to the Law of God as that expert in Hebrew Scriptures could hope to match the kindness (undeserved love in action) of the fictional Samaritan. In the end, however, that is the Law's demand and Christ's instruction. Ultimately, Christ becomes a Good Samaritan for us by His perfect fulfilling of even the most rigorous demands of the Law (Galatians 4:4–5).

78. In the story, a priest and a Levite pass by the injured man. Most likely they recognized the possibility that the robbers left him in the road as bait, hoping to draw into their trap additional victims. In any case, helping the injured man would have cost them time and money. Since he was a stranger to them, why bother?

79. We can measure the kindness of the Samaritan by recognizing the risk he took (the injured man could be bait), the immediate expense that he incurred (first aid medications), the expense to which he committed himself at the inn (two silver coins plus whatever else the innkeeper decided to charge him later), and the inconvenience of interrupting his journey. In anticipation of the last part of this study, the session leader might ask the class participants how we would measure God's kindness.

80. In an effort to help make the size and nature of the Samaritan's kindness more apparent, the leader might ask the participants if they can think of any modern parallels to this story. During the discussion, the leader should explore the pros and cons of helping strangers today. The risks are very real for anyone who extends a helping hand. In addition to all the risks and expenses in the story, modern Good Samaritans may risk a lawsuit or other legal action when they stop to help.

81. Since God's standard is impossibly high for sinners, we need to recognize that none can justify themselves on the Last Day before the Judge of all by their works. Only through faith in Christ, the true Good Samaritan, can we hope to be saved. Nevertheless, kindness continues to mark the life of the child of God, not as an effort to earn salvation, but as a faith-filled response of thankfulness and a fruit of the indwelling Holy Spirit.

Sheep and Goats

The session leader may need to clear up a couple of misunderstandings about this story before beginning the lesson. First, note that the sheep and goats are separated before any deeds of kindness are mentioned. We understand from the rest of Scripture that salvation comes as a free gift through faith in Jesus Christ. The previous separation of sheep from goats reflects the fact that the eternal destiny of the people in the story has already been decided. The leader might talk about the fact that a person faces judgment at the time of death and enters heaven or hell immediately (as reflected in the story of Lazarus and the rich man, Luke 16:19–31, and the criminal on the cross next to Jesus, Luke 23:39–43). The end of this age culminates in the resurrection of all people and the public judgment of all humanity. Jesus has this public judgment in mind when He tells the story of the sheep and the goats. The leader may want to emphasize that neither the sheep nor the goats are surprised at their eternal destiny. Their remarks indicate their amazement at the *reason* for the Judge's decision. Matthew makes this more obvious in the original language of the Gospel (Greek) as those who hear the judgment say, "when *You* did we see . . . ?" The addition of "You" and its position in the sentence indicate emphasis for the reader. What people do to Christians ("brothers of mine"), Christ Jesus takes personally.

82. The phrase "Son of Man" refers, of course, to Jesus. He applies this to Himself, with Daniel 7:13–14 in mind, when standing trial before Caiaphas (Mark 14:62). The title designates the eschatological Judge of all who wields the authority of God Himself and creates an everlasting kingdom of all peoples. Remember that Jesus has authority to forgive sins (Mark 2:10) and to decide what is and what is not permitted on the Sabbath (Mark 2:25–28). In fact, "all authority in heaven and on earth" has been given to Him (Matthew 28:18).

83. Indications that we are saved by grace through faith in Christ Jesus alone include the fact that separation occurs before the Judge presents the evidence (or lack of evidence) for the existence of saving faith; the fact that He describes the sheep as "blessed by My Father" (Matthew 25:34), a grace statement; and the fact that the kingdom into which they enter has been prepared for them since the beginning of the world (see Ephesians 1:3–14; Romans 8:28–30).

84. The kind acts done by the sheep reveal their living faith but do not provide the reason for or the cause of their salvation.

85. The acts of kindness mentioned by the Judge show love in action, a fulfillment of Leviticus 19:18 ("love your neighbor as yourself") but with an added twist—these acts have all been done to fellow believers, including the least important brothers of Jesus.

The session leader can point out an Old Testament precedent for Jesus taking personally what people do to Christians. In Genesis 9:6, God establishes the legal requirement for the execution of murderers based on the fact that God created man in His own image. Therefore a human being represents God, and an attack on such a representative constitutes an attack on God Himself. The leader can make an even stronger point when discussing Matthew 25 by reminding the participants that Christians form the body of Christ (1 Corinthians 12) and He is our Head (Ephesians 4:15; 5:23; Colossians 1:18). Jesus rules over all creation as Lord, but He has a special, personal, intimate relationship with believers.

86. The session leader has an excellent opportunity to make a point that people don't often hear. It appears that the goats face damnation because they failed to be nice to Christians. Their lack of kindness, however, to the brothers and sisters of Christ publicly reveals the real reason for their fate: they did not trust in Christ for salvation. Their lack of saving faith shows up in the absence of the fruit of the Spirit (Galatians 5:22–23). For their lack of faith in Him who died and rose for all people, the goats end up with the devil and his angels.

87. God originally created hell for Satan and the angels who rebelled with him against God. Unbelievers end up there because they do not trust in Jesus for their salvation. Lack of saving faith, revealed by an absence of kind actions to Christians, condemns that person to share the fate of the devil and his angels. The session leader might take this opportunity to talk about the importance of missions and witness, bringing Christ to the nations and our neighbors, since so very much is at stake. Remember the church's Great Commission (Matthew 28:18–20) and His promise to make us His witnesses (Acts 1:8)!

The Gospel Spreads

Luke offers us a basic outline of Acts in 1:8 and traces the Gospel's advance from Jerusalem to Rome. In chapters 3–4, he relates the story of the crippled beggar who had looked for a handout from Peter and John but received healing instead.

88. Luke does not mention the man's faith prior to the healing. Perhaps this highlights the awesome power of Jesus' name in this miracle.

89. Like the man in Acts 3–4, the man in John 5:1–5 is about forty and had been unable to walk for a long time. As in Acts 3–4, the crippled man does not offer any evidence of faith prior to the healing. Unlike the beggar in Acts 3–4, however, the man in John 5 seems to have no faith in Jesus even after the healing. Jesus confronts him with dire words of warning in 5:14, and he informs the authorities about Jesus in the very next verse. Contrast the behavior of the crippled beggar in Acts 3–4 who can't seem to let go of Peter and John, holding on to them while walking and jumping and praising God. Naturally, this draws quite a crowd.

90. Peter takes the opportunity to preach the second Christian sermon. (The first was on Pentecost, recorded in Acts 2. Through the Word of God, the number of baptized believers grew by about three thousand.) The session leader could point out to the participants the strong Law/Gospel content of Peter's sermon.

91. God used this sermon (and later the Sacrament of Baptism) as an act of kindness to bring salvation to people, a pattern we have seen in the Old Testament section as well. Kindness may be defined as underserved love in action with an ultimate goal of salvation through the name of Jesus. This is important because only Jesus saves people from their sins (Acts 4:12).

The Lame Are Healed

Paul traveled from A.D. 46–48 through modern south-central Turkey bringing the Gospel to Gentiles at the direction of the church at Antioch. The text of Acts 13:1–3 actually mentions Barnabas first, and he appears to be the more important of the two travelers (at least for a little while). The session leader may want to point out that Saul of Tarsus never changed his name to Paul. He would have had both from birth. We read of Saul as early as Acts 7:58, where he witnesses Stephen's martyrdom. The Lord Jesus confronts and converts him in chapter 9 (roughly A.D. 35). Eleven years later Luke still refers to him as Saul (13:1–9a). Luke introduces us to one of his Roman names (as a citizen he would have had three) in 13:9b and consistently refers to him as Paul after that.

92. The leader will want to highlight the fact that the faith of the crippled man plays an important role here. His faith came by hearing the Word of God that Paul preached (for a summary see Acts 13:13–47), a point Paul makes in Romans 10:17. Through the Gospel the Holy Spirit

draws people to faith in Jesus Christ. He uses a variety of preparatory tools at His disposal—including acts of kindness.

93. Note how differently the pagan townspeople reacted to this miracle when compared to the common Jewish reaction in Acts 3. Instead of praising God and turning to Jesus, they mistake Barnabas and Paul for pagan gods. We see here a glimpse of the difficulty in cross-cultural ministry!

94. Paul stops the sacrifice and uses the opportunity to announce the kindness of the one true God—the Holy Trinity—in showering rain on their crops and giving them food for their stomachs and joy for their hearts (14:17). This verse reveals something of the inclusive nature of God's kindness and the breadth of His care even for unbelievers ("satisfying your hearts with food and gladness").

95. The crowd, swayed by hostile Jewish elements from other cities, stones Paul and leaves him for dead. It may be that his survival is a miracle from God, given the fact that he had been stoned, was left for dead, and then got up on his own power and went back into the city (14:20). We cannot make too much of it, however, since Luke does not give us more detail. Remember that kindness takes risks. Even if it is true that "no good deed goes unpunished," we must not cease to do acts of kindness for the sake of the Gospel.

Christ the Ideal

96. Earlier in this session we noticed God's active kindness toward us shown in Titus 3:3–8. We revisit this passage, noting the connection between kindness and love. We have defined kindness as "undeserved love in action," and we can see this no place more clearly than Christ crucified and risen for us. Paul speaks of the kindness and love (literally "philanthropy") of God in 3:4. We might say that kindness (the practical deed) flows from love for people (the attitude of God in Christ). Both appeared when Jesus became incarnate and was born, incarnate Love who came to do the ultimate act of kindness (the cross). The session leader may want to summarize the things we have learned about kindness in this two-part study.

97. Kindness flows from underserved love. We might define it as "applied love." Kindness includes all people, regardless of faith, color, sex, or nationality. Kindness takes risks, setting aside the welfare of the self for the welfare of the neighbor. Ultimately, kindness points to Christ. The Holy Spirit uses kind deeds to exhibit compassion toward

people and, when and where it pleases Him, prepares them to hear the Gospel. That we are brought to faith through God's Word and Spirit is itself God's kindness in action toward us.

98. God's kindness comes to us, of course, as a free gift of grace through the life, death, and resurrection of Jesus Christ. Jesus applied God's love to people throughout His ministry and "cut the covenant" (remember the lesson of David and Jonathan—kindness binds people together) in His own blood on the cross. We participate in the blessings of that covenant by eating His flesh and drinking His blood in the Lord's Supper (Matthew 26:26–28; 1 Corinthians 11:23–26).

99. In Baptism, we are buried with Christ in His death and raised with Him in His resurrection to a new life (see Romans 6:1–4). Paul has in mind both our justification (that God declares us right with Him through faith in Christ alone) and our sanctification (that the Holy Spirit leads us into a new lifestyle typified by the fruit of the Spirit).

100. At our Baptism the Holy Spirit created a new person through water and the Word ("regeneration" see also John 3:1 6) and made us citizens of Christ's eternal, glorious kingdom ("renewal"). The session leader may want to share with the participants that the original Greek word behind "renewal" appears only one other place in the New Testament, Matthew 19:28 ("renewal," NIV; "new world," ESV; "regeneration," KJV). In that passage Jesus uses the word to refer to His postresurrection kingdom into which believers are welcomed on the Last Day. In our Baptism, God applied His great love for us by providing us a new birth now and a glorious inheritance at the return of Jesus, who comes to judge the living and the dead.

5

Goodness and Grace

Objectives

By the power of the Holy Spirit working through God's Word, participants will

- appreciate the holistic use of the word *goodness* in the Bible;
- understand that God is the source of all goodness;
- learn that human beings cannot define goodness apart from God's will;
- see in Christ the ultimate Goodness of God for us.

The early chapters of Genesis introduce us to God, man, and sin. Chapter 3 especially explains the predicament human beings face from conception and birth, revealing the origin of suffering and death. The session leader can direct the attention of the participants to the tree of the knowledge of good and evil appearing first in Genesis 2:9, 17 and playing a pivotal role in the temptation narrative of 3:1–6.

The leader might point out that Eve thought the fruit of the tree was "good for food" (3:6) and ask the participants if she was right or not. God created all things and called all His creation "good," even "very good" (Genesis 1:31). Only the lack of man's helper was "not good" (2:18), and God soon took care of that problem.

101. The fruit was "good" because it was God's creation, but it was not "good" for Eve and Adam to eat because of God's prohibition. God alone is good and His revealed will—His Word—is the sole criterion for determining what is good. Thus, for Adam and Eve the results of eating the prohibited fruit were not good.

Our Good Shepherd

102. Participants are asked to list separately the physical and spiritual blessings in this psalm. Some are clearly physical: green pastures and quiet waters. One speaks directly to our emotional well-being: "He restores my soul" (v. 3).

103. Verse 4 strikes us as very spiritual, leading us through the valley of death safely (other interpretations are also possible). Both the beginning and ending of the psalm seem holistic, that is, they treat people as whole persons (body and soul together). "I shall not want" (v. 1) embraces the whole of our lives, as does the last verse: "goodness and mercy shall follow me all the days of my life" (v. 6).

104. Participants are asked to define goodness. Hopefully they will wrestle with the assignment without developing a firm answer just yet. Certainly goodness embraces physical and spiritual blessings in this psalm, and the leader may want to leave it at that for now.

The Covenant Connection

Psalm 23:5–6 includes covenant elements that help us understand God's gracious attitude towards us. He pours out His goodness upon us because He has promised to do so. He bound Himself to His love for His people by establishing covenants with them, as He has done in Christ Jesus for us. The session leader may want to refer participants to the "Major Covenants in the Old Testament" in the *Concordia Self-Study Bible*, page 18.

2 Samuel 7:8–16 stands as a major covenant in the Old Testament. David wanted to build a temple for the Lord, but the Lord forbade it. Instead, God promised to build a "house" for him.

105. God reminded David that He made him Israel's king and defeated David's enemies (7:8–9a).

106. God promised to make David's reputation and role in the plan of salvation very large ("will make for you a great name," 7:9b).

107. God promised to provide a permanent place for His people (7:10). The Messianic part of the covenant between the Lord and David appears in 7:11b–16. The "house" God promises to build for David is the Christ, and the eternal throne mentioned in verse 16 is Jesus' eternal kingdom. Psalm 110 (frequently quoted in the New Testament) presents a picture of this King and His everlasting kingdom.

108. David's focus in Psalm 27, however, clearly falls on the part of the covenant where God protected him from his enemies.

109. In Psalm 27:13 the "goodness of the LORD" refers to God's covenant faithfulness as exhibited in the defeat and destruction of David's enemies.

The Glory of the Lord

Deuteronomy 33 offers us a remarkable picture of God's goodness as He deals with Israel and with Moses, His servant. God warns Moses in the early verses of the chapter that He will send an angel to lead Israel because God might get angry with them and destroy them if He led them (33:3). The people rebel against God, it seems, at every opportunity (see the incident of the golden calf in ch. 32). Their sin, like that of Moses, cannot be denied. Aaron and Israel made the golden calf and worshiped it, a sin of idolatry (Exodus 32). Moses struck the rock at Meribah when he had been commanded only to speak to it, a failure of trust in God and a violation of God's holiness (Numbers 20:6–13). For this sin, God did not allow Moses to enter the Promised Land (Deuteronomy 34, especially v. 4). God's fellowship with Moses is founded upon God's grace, a love deserved neither by the nation nor by its most eminent leader.

110. Moses has amazing confidence before the Lord. In Exodus 33:12, he voices his objection to God's plan to send an angel to lead the people in the wilderness. God responds (v. 14) by agreeing to lead the people Himself, accompanying Moses.

111. What gave Moses such confidence? God's own promise and gracious love (33:12b–13). Moses based his relationship on God's own Word and stood firm on that Word even in front of the Lord Himself!

112. Moses asks to see God's glory (33:18).

113. The Lord responds to Moses' request by stating that He will reveal His goodness and proclaim His name to him (33:19–20).

The session leader might talk about the connection between the two concepts. Both reveal God's nature and attributes and communicate something essential about God. The best place to define glory is at the cross. Jesus does that in John 12:23–33. God reveals His glory chiefly in the incarnation, life, crucifixion, death, and resurrection of Jesus Christ. The leader can help the students make the connection between glory and the salvation of sinners.

114. To peer into or to be exposed to God's essence or nature unmitigated by His forgiveness, love, and grace is to invite certain death. In His nature God is most holy and all-powerful. In order for us to "see"

Him as He is, He must clothe Himself in human flesh (John 1:14, 18; see also Matthew 17:1–8).

115. Exodus 33:19 should help participants understand God's goodness. God defines His goodness as (1) the proclamation of His name ("the LORD" represents the Hebrew "I AM" of Exodus 3:14) and (2) showing mercy and compassion on sinners.

6

Goodness and God

Objectives

By the power of the Holy Spirit working through God's Word, participants will
- understand the critical importance of God's revealed will for us in distinguishing what is genuinely good;
- appreciate God's holy Law, which reveals His perfect will for our lives;
- begin to identify specific ways we may exercise the fruit of patience, kindness, and goodness towards family, friends, coworkers, and even strangers;
- rejoice in Christ, who fulfilled the Law perfectly for us and took the punishment we deserved for breaking the Law, thus saving us by His grace.

116. On a human level we use different criteria for determining whether or not practically anything is good. Ask any three-year-old whether spinach is good and you probably will not be surprised by the answer. The label *good,* as we apply it in our daily lives, depends oftentimes on whether or not we like someone or something. Psalm 34:8 reminds us that, ultimately, "The LORD is good." He alone determines what is good and what is evil. Practically anything He has created and determined "good" (Genesis 1, especially v. 31) can be abused and become bad for us. But even in such cases, the Lord's forgiving goodness is palpable—it can be "tasted"—in the One whose body was broken for us, but whose bones remained untouched (Psalm 34:8, 20).

God and Good

The session leader will use this part of the study to help the participants see the connection between God's will and goodness. In Matthew 4:1–4, the evangelist records the first temptation of Jesus by Satan. After forty days and nights without food, Jesus hungered (talk about an understatement!). Satan merely suggested He use His divine power to make bread out of rocks. No harm in that, is there? Daily bread must be a good thing because Jesus teaches us to pray for it in the Lord's Prayer. The critical factor for Jesus (and for us), though, is whether God wants us to have bread or not.

117. Exodus 16:1–4 reveals a complaining and self-centered attitude on the part of God's people. They failed the test of trust, just as Adam and Eve had failed the test in Genesis 3:1–6. God provided bread (manna) for them, but their lack of faith would lead to many problems in the years ahead. Nevertheless, their complaints often centered around food.

118. In Numbers 11, the people complained about the monotony of manna each and every day. They wanted variety and diversity in their diet, something everyone can understand. The problem was their attitude, showing a lack of trust in the Lord and a disobedience to His will.

119. Deuteronomy 8:2–3 explains that the Lord withheld food from the Israelites to test them and to humble them. He wanted to teach them to rely on Him in faith, not on the bread and meat that they could see. It's easy to trust God when we have everything we want, but can we trust Him when we don't have what we think we need?

120. Daily bread is a fine thing in and of itself. However, if God wills us to go without it, then bread becomes a bad thing. God's will determines what is good and what is not. Jesus chose to resist bread in order to fulfill His Father's will. In His obedience He was the perfect Israelite, the perfect man: one who fully submits to His Father.

121. Israel, like Adam and Eve, chose unbelief and disobedience. Ironically, these tests involved food—by itself a gift of God. Jesus is the new and perfect Adam (Romans 5:12–21; 1 Corinthians 15:22) and the new and perfect Israelite. Jesus' 40-day temptation compares to Israel's 40-year wilderness experience. Jesus' selections of passages from Deuteronomy (specifically 8:3; 6:16; and 6:13) are used to successfully rebuke the devil. This contrasts to Israel's frequent failures in faith and morals, which will be shown repeatedly in her subsequent history.

122. Jesus quotes Deuteronomy 8:3 to drive home the point (based on God's Word) that God's will determines what is good and what is not. For Jesus in the wilderness, God's will was simple—no bread. The Word was His real food (see also John 4:34).

God's Law and Gospel

The Law of God reflects His holiness and reveals His will for His people. As such, it is good through and through. However, when we come into contact with it we die. The Law kills us because we are sinners (recall God's statement that no one can see His face and live, Exodus 33:20). As Paul wrestles with the question of the Law in the Christian life under the cross, he makes a number of disturbing points.

123. Sin uses the Law to produce more sin. Paul uses the example of coveting. Coveting something or someone would not count as a sin if no law condemned it. Ironically, the Law itself serves as sin's "base camp" of operations to increase itself in our lives (7:7–8).

124. The Law kills precisely because it is an expression of the living God. Paul challenges us to reconsider ourselves. We like to think of ourselves as good people. But the Law, reflecting God's holiness and righteousness, inevitably kills us. After looking in the mirror of the Law, we confess that we are not good at all.

125. Paul affirms that the Law of God is holy because God Himself is holy. Further, Paul argues that God's commandments that make up the Law are "holy and righteous and good" (7:12). The session leader might take the time to point out that good is what God wills and does regardless of our judgment on it. We make the same mistake as Adam and Eve when we declare something "good" or "bad" without first seeing what God's Word says about it.

126. God gave the Law to Moses to guide the people in their lives as His servants. He had already saved them in the exodus, so it was obvious that salvation came by grace, not works. Human beings start out life as little sinners, revealing the self-centeredness and self-involvement that stand as the hallmarks of original sin. The Law serves two purposes at this point: it condemns sin as sin, showing us clearly that we cannot earn God's love nor His salvation; it completely removes any pretense from sin, showing it to be utterly wrong. The session leader could ask participants to offer examples of how we try to make sin look righteous apart from God's law (adultery, homosexuality, greed, theft, etc.). The

Law paves the way for the Gospel by showing our utterly hopeless condition under God's righteous and holy judgment.

127. Victory over sin, death, and the grave comes to Paul and to us as a blessed and joyful gift of God through Jesus Christ our Lord (7:24–25). The session leader may want to spend time and talk about the consolation and power God gives us in Christ through the means of grace (Word and Sacraments). Through these God not only forgives and comforts us, but also gives us the ability to live godly lives. This will help the participants move into the next section.

Practical Goodness

The session leader might introduce the participants to the concept that worship extends beyond the walls of the church. God reaches out to His people through Word and Sacrament, and we respond with prayer, praise, and thanksgiving. But it does not end there. Worship continues outside in vocation—wherever God has placed us. Therefore, the liturgical act of sacrifice serves admirably to describe the entire Christian life. God calls us to set ourselves aside for Him and to place the needs of others ahead of ourselves. In this way we become "living sacrifices," a "logical" (sometimes translated "spiritual") act of worship (Romans 12:1).

128. We cannot transform our minds. Only God can accomplish that. He does so by pouring out on us His Holy Spirit. Through Word and Sacrament the Spirit brings forth and sustains a new person in Christ Jesus (see Ephesians 4:23–24; Colossians 3:10; Titus 3:5). Throughout the rest of our lives that new person struggles with the old sinful self to see things God's way rather than our own way.

129. The attitude imparted by the Holy Spirit is Christlike humility. The best place to unpack this new attitude is Philippians 2:5–11, where Christ Himself serves as the model.

130. Paul uses the body metaphor. This metaphor is expanded upon further in 1 Corinthians 12. We are here for each other, not just ourselves. At this point, the session leader can guide the participants in discussing how the gifts they listed can benefit that fellowship.

131. Answers may vary. The session leader should encourage participants to express their thoughts on which of the directives in 12:9–21 challenge them the most.

Christ the Ideal

We see goodness incarnate in Jesus. Jesus enjoys a right relationship with God, full of trust and obedience. He fulfills the Law of God and yet dies the death of the ultimate lawbreaker on the cross. Far more than the Righteous One, we see at the cross of Christ Jesus the goodness of God working out our salvation.

132. Jesus confronts the rich young man with the Law. The young man thought he had kept it, but he had not even scratched the surface.

Jesus reveals the fuller extent of the Law by telling him to keep the commandments, sell all his possessions and give the proceeds to the poor, and follow Him. As impossible as it sounds for us, the session leader might point out that Jesus did even more than this by giving up the glory of heaven to become a human being and ultimately go to the cross (see again Philippians 2:5–11). This He did for us!

133. Apparently, some people in Jesus' day thought that rich people had the best chance of earning salvation. If the rich cannot be saved by works, then no one can (18:26). A camel (proverbially the largest animal) has a better chance of going through the eye of a needle (proverbially the smallest opening) unharmed than even the best or most privileged of us has of earning salvation.

134. In 18:27, Jesus clearly has the cross in mind.

135. God also graciously provides gifts in this life and in the next for His children (18:29–30). The family of faith welcomes all who leave their earthly family for the sake of the Gospel.

The session leader will want to avoid a "health and wealth" gospel that promises an easy and comfortable life here on earth for God's people. The opposite is quite often the case. Nevertheless, we praise God for the many, many good gifts He provides for us—chiefly, salvation and eternal life, but also including our daily bread.

Glossary

calling. See **vocation.**

covenant. A relationship or agreement not based on kinship. A contract. A "parity" covenant is an agreement between equals. A "suzerain" covenant is an agreement between a lord and his servant or between a strong nation and a weak nation.

double predestination. The false teaching that God eternally decreed who is to be saved and who is to be damned (with no hope of repentance).

election. From the Latin word "to choose." The biblical teaching that God chose believers through Christ to be His people and to inherit eternal life. God chose them purely by grace and not because of their good works or their faith.

fruit of the Spirit. Effects produced in believers by the indwelling of the Holy Spirit (Galatians 5:22–23). The good works produced by faith in Christ.

fear of the Lord. Reverence and trust in the Lord.

Gospel. The message of Christ's death and resurrection for the forgiveness of sins. The Holy Spirit works through the Gospel to create faith and convert people.

holistic. Applying to a whole subject. In theology, teaching that applies to a person as a whole instead of focusing solely on the spiritual or physical aspect of a person.

holy. Set apart for a divine purpose (e.g., Holy Scripture is set apart from all other types of writing). The Holy Spirit makes Christians holy (see **sanctification**).

justification. God declares sinners to be just, or righteous, for Christ's sake; that is, God has imputed or charged our sins to Christ, and He imputes or credits Christ's righteousness to us.

kinsman-redeemer. A person responsible for protecting vulnerable family members, especially in areas of inheritance.

Law. God's will that shows people how they should live (e.g., the Ten Commandments) and condemns their failure. The preaching of the Law is the cause of contrition.

parity. See **covenant.**

repentance. Sorrow for sin caused by the condemnation of the Law. Sometimes the word *repentance* is used in a broad way to describe all of conversion, including faith in God's mercy.

Sacrament. Literally, "something sacred." In the Lutheran church a sacrament is a sacred act that (1) was instituted by God, (2) has a visible element, and (3) offers the forgiveness of sins earned by Christ. The sacraments include Baptism, the Lord's Supper, and Absolution (if one counts the pastor as the visible element; see Apology XII, 41; XIII, 3–5; Large Catechism IV, 74).

sanctification. The spiritual growth that follows justification by grace through faith in Christ.

Semitic. From the Hebrew name *Shem*, who was an ancestor of the Jewish people and other Middle Eastern groups (Genesis 10:1, 21–31). A word used to distinguish the descendants of Shem and their culture (e.g., Hebrew is a *Semitic* language).

suzerain. See **covenant.**

theology of glory. The idea that the true knowledge of God comes from the study of nature, which reflects God's glory. Also, the belief that suffering should not be part of the Christian life because God's people always triumph.

vocation. From the Latin word for "calling." A person's occupation or duties before God. For example, a person may serve as a father, a husband, and an engineer. Each "calling" comes with different responsibilities.